FOSSIL FILES

MARINE FOSSILS

HEATHER MOORE NIVER

PowerKiDS
press

NEW YORK

Published in 2017 by The Rosen Publishing Group, Inc.
29 East 21st Street, New York, NY 10010

First Edition

Editor: Melissa Raé Shofner
Book Design: Tanya Dellaccio

Photo Credits: Cover John Cancalosi/Getty Images; cover, back cover, p. 1 Victoria Kalinina; p. 5 Jixin YU/Shutterstock.com; p. 7 (rippled fossils) Auscape/Universal Images Group/Getty Images; p. 7 (ammonites) MarcelClemens/Shutterstock.com; p. 9 David Lade/Shutterstock.com; p. 11 (horseshoe crab) Nipon-Photo/Shutterstock.com; p. 11 (trilobite) I love photo/Shutterstockcom; p. 13 (shark tooth), (Cretaceous shark tooth) mj007/Shutterstock.com; p. 13 (megalodon rendering) Herschel Hoffmeyer/Shutterstock.com; p. 15 DEA/G. CIGOLINI/De Agostini/Getty Images; p. 17 mantisdesign/Shutterstock.com; p. 19 De Agostini Picture Library/Getty Images; p. 20 Stukkey/ Shutterstock.com; p. 21 (fossils) Insights/Universal Images Group/Getty Images; p. 21 (illustration) https:// commons.wikimedia.org/wiki/File:Basilosaurus.jpg; p. 23 (plesiosaurs rendering) Mark Stevenson/ Stocktrek Images/Getty Images; p. 23 (pteranodon fossil) https://commons.wikimedia.org/wiki/ File:Pteranodon_sp_AMNH_7515.jpg; p. 25 FPG/Hulton Archive/Getty Images; p. 27 (nurse shark) Andrea Izzotti/Shutterstock.com; p. 27 (Ptychodus rendering) https://commons.wikimedia.org/wiki/ File:Ptychodus1.jpg; p. 29 (tylosaurus rendering) Michael Rosskothen/Shutterstock.com; p. 29 (Mosasaurus teeth) Garry Gay/Getty Images.

Library of Congress Cataloging-in-Publication Data

Names: Niver, Heather Moore.
Title: Marine fossils / Heather Moore Niver.
Description: New York : PowerKids Press, [2017] | Series: Fossil files |
  Includes index.
Identifiers: LCCN 2016045958| ISBN 9781499427424 (pbk. book) | ISBN
  9781508152729 (6 pack) | ISBN 9781499428568 (library bound book)
Subjects: LCSH: Marine animals, Fossil–Juvenile literature. | Fishes,
  Fossil–Juvenile literature. | Fossils–Juvenile literature.
Classification: LCC QE766 .N58 2017 | DDC 560/.457–dc23
LC record available at https://lccn.loc.gov/2016045958

Manufactured in the United States of America

CPSIA Compliance Information: Batch Batch #BW17PK: For Further Information contact Rosen Publishing, New York, New York at 1-800-237-9932

CONTENTS

Finding Fossils 4

Fossils Large and Small 6

Way Down in the Water 8

Casts and Molds 10

Shark Tooth Fossils 12

An Amazing Discovery 14

Coral Beds 16

On the Land, In the Sea 18

Desert Surprises 20

Marine Fossils in Kansas? 22

A Fish Within a Fish 24

Shell-Crushing Shark 26

The First Marine Herbivore 28

Studying Marine Fossils 30

Glossary 31

Index 32

Websites 32

FINDING FOSSILS

Fossils are the preserved remains of plants and animals that lived many years ago. They're found in Earth's crust and offer clues about what life on Earth was like long ago. Sometimes only part of an **organism** is fossilized. Other times an entire organism is preserved. Scientists called paleontologists study fossils to learn about the past.

Marine fossils are important because they show scientists where there was once water on Earth. Sometimes these places come as a big surprise. For instance, would you guess there was once an ocean over the state of Kansas? Water once also covered the rocks that now form the world's highest mountains. Scientists have found the fossils of marine organisms in these places. Keep reading for more magnificent marine fossil finds.

Dig It!

Woolly mammoth teeth are some of the youngest, or most recent, fossils found on Earth. Fossils of large bacteria that lived around 3 billion years ago are some of the oldest.

Paleontology

Paleontology is the study of the fossils of plants and animals that lived many years ago. Scientists who study ancient life-forms and their fossils are known as paleontologists. Paleontologists carefully remove fossils from the earth and take notes on everything about them. They record where they found fossils and how they made these discoveries. Observations made by paleontologists help us understand how a prehistoric organism may have lived and why it may have died.

Some of the world's oldest fossils are marine fossils. These fossils belong to organisms such as the cyanobacteria seen on this river.

FOSSILS LARGE AND SMALL

A body fossil can be the preserved remains of a whole organism, or it might just be part of one. Body fossils may be bones, shells, feathers, or leaves. An organism's preserved tracks or waste are called trace fossils. Trace fossils show the activity of an organism.

Some fossils are so small you need a microscope to see them. These are called microfossils. Preserved bacteria and **algae** are microfossils. Macrofossils, on the other hand, are large enough to be viewed without using a microscope.

Fossils are often found in layers of rock deep below Earth's surface. Marine fossils are found in areas that are or were at one point covered with water. They've been found on every continent on Earth.

Dig It!

"Fossil' comes from the Latin word *fossilis*, which means "dug up."

Oceans Everywhere!

Most of Earth's surface was once covered by water. We know this because marine fossils have been found in the Himalayas, the Alps, and the Rocky Mountains. Finding marine fossils in mountains tells scientists that the stones of these towering peaks were once underwater. Ammonites provide an example of a marine fossil found in the mountains. Their fossilized spiral-shaped shells have been found in the Himalayas in the country of Nepal. Today, the Himalayas are the highest mountains on Earth.

Scientists have found preserved ripples in the ancient seafloor. This billion-year-old rock is located in Barraranna Gorge in south Australia.

WAY DOWN IN THE WATER

Large bodies of water, such as oceans, are the perfect places for fossils to be created. When an organism dies in the ocean, it may be quickly covered with sediment. Sediment is rocks, sand, and stones that have been moved and deposited by wind, water, or glaciers.

Sediment in cold, calm waters at the bottom of a deep ocean protects an organism's remains from being eaten or **decomposing**. These conditions are the reason paleontologists find so many marine fossils. The sooner the remains are covered, the better the chances that they'll be preserved as a fossil.

Fossils may also be created when an organism's remains are trapped in ice, resin, or tar. Scientists have found all sorts of prehistoric creatures preserved like this—from tiny ants to entire mammoths.

As layers of sediment pile on top of each other, the remains of organisms are covered up and may become fossilized. Here you can see many marine fossils in different layers of rock.

Figuring Out Fossils

To be considered a fossil, an organism's preserved remains need to be at least 10,000 years old. Recent fossils are from the Holocene epoch, which started about 11,700 years ago. An epoch is a division of time in geology that lasts a few million years. Some fossils are close to 4 billion years old. These fossils are from the Archaean eon (4 billion to 2.5 billion years ago). An eon is the largest division of time in geology. One eon lasts hundreds of millions of years.

CASTS AND MOLDS

Marine fossils sometimes form through a process called casting. This means that when an ancient marine organism died, its remains sank to the seafloor and became buried in sediment. Over time, the remains rotted away and left an empty space called a mold in the sedimentary rock. Water flowing through the sediment carried minerals, which filled in the shape of the mold. Over time, the minerals hardened into what is called a cast. Shallow casts are called imprints. These were often left by prehistoric plant leaves.

Trilobites were shelled marine animals that lived between 521 million and 240 million years ago. These creatures lived in seas all over the planet and ranged in size from about .4 to 27.6 inches (1 to 70 cm). Trilobites had hard shells that were perfect for creating casts and molds.

trilobite fossil

Trilobites are distant relatives of modern horseshoe crabs. What similarities do you see?

horseshoe crab

SHARK TOOTH FOSSILS

Paleontologists have learned a lot about prehistoric sharks by studying their fossilized teeth. By looking at these teeth, they discovered that megalodon was the largest shark to ever have lived. Fossilized teeth also reveal what these prehistoric sharks ate and where they lived. The largest megalodon tooth found is 7.4 inches (18.8 cm) long.

It's easy for paleontologists to study ancient sharks because there are so many fossilized shark teeth. Sharks lose thousands of teeth throughout their lives. Their teeth also fossilize easily. When a tooth falls out, it sinks to the ocean floor and is covered in sediment. Water makes its way through the sediment and minerals slowly replace part of the tooth. This process, called permineralization, takes thousands of years.

This shark tooth is about 45 million years old and is likely from an **ancestor** of megalodon. Paleontologists believe megalodon lived in coastal waters 28 million to about 1.6 million years ago.

rendering of a megalodon

Dig It!

Scientists believe megalodon could grow to be between 50 and 60 feet (15.2 to 18.3 m) long. Great white sharks only grow to be about 21 feet (6.4 m) long.

fossilized shark tooth

AN AMAZING DISCOVERY

Some ancient marine animals had hard outer coverings or shells. These creatures were more likely to become fossils because the hard parts of their bodies decomposed slowly. The remains of soft-bodied marine animals were more likely to break down before they could be preserved.

However, in 2009, paleontologists found more than 1,500 fossils of soft-bodied marine animals in Morocco. The fossils included those of sponges, mollusks, and worms that lived between 480 and 472 million years ago. These fossils suggest that soft-bodied marine creatures appeared on Earth 30 million years earlier than scientists originally believed. They also tell us that certain soft-bodied marine animals didn't go extinct, or die out, during the Cambrian period (541 million to 485.5 million years ago) as had previously been thought.

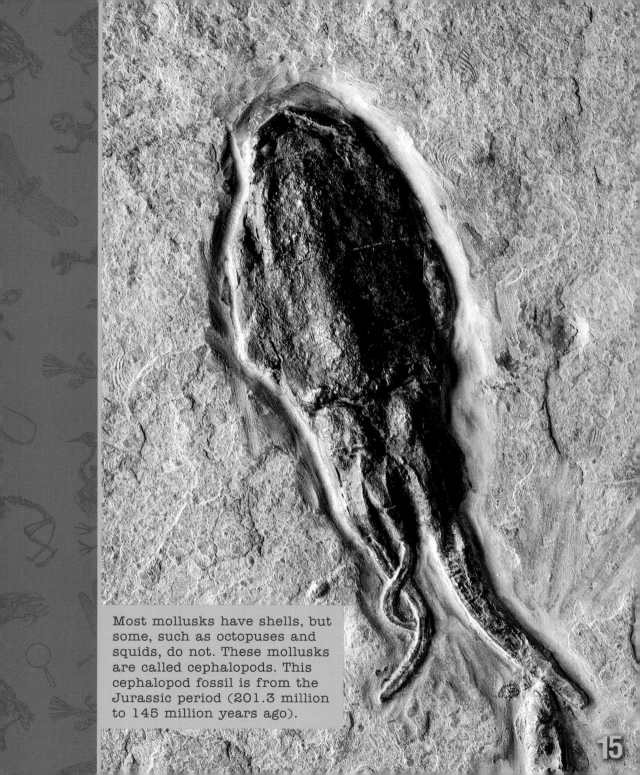

Most mollusks have shells, but some, such as octopuses and squids, do not. These mollusks are called cephalopods. This cephalopod fossil is from the Jurassic period (201.3 million to 145 million years ago).

CORAL BEDS

Corals are soft-bodied marine animals that have many tentacles, or arms. Corals are interesting because their skeleton is like rock. When corals die, their soft bodies rot away but their hard skeletons are left behind. Modern corals live in big groups called colonies. Their skeletons form a large structure called a coral reef. Some ancient corals also lived in colonies, but some lived alone. The skeletons of both types have been preserved as fossils.

Some of the most famous coral fossils are found in the Falls of the Ohio State Park in Indiana. Millions of coral fossils can be found here, but they can't be removed. These special fossil beds, which extend into Kentucky, are closely protected.

Dig It!

"Rugose" means wrinkled or rough. The outer surface of most Rugosa corals looked wrinkly. This order of corals is now extinct.

This Rugosa coral fossil was found in Australia in rock from the Permian period. It may be anywhere from 298.9 million to 252.2 million years old.

A Puzzling Question

When paleontologists first discovered marine fossils on land, they guessed that land fossils might be found in the land beneath the seas. The more they learned about fossils, however, the more they realized that this wasn't true. Marine fossils are found on land, but the fossils of land animals are not found under modern seas. Sea levels have changed over time, but the seafloors we know today were never actually areas of dry land.

ON THE LAND, IN THE SEA

Until recently, certain kinds of **frond**-shaped organisms were believed to have lived in the sea millions of years ago. Their fossils have been found in rock that scientists thought formed from ancient seafloor sediment. However, new studies suggest that this rock may actually be the remains of early soil. This means that some fossils that were believed to be marine may actually belong to organisms that lived on land.

Scientists are working hard to sort through the details of this soil mystery. Figuring out where and when fossils formed is an important part of figuring out when organisms began to live on land. This new soil discovery could mean that life on Earth moved from the sea to the land up to 100 million years sooner than scientists originally thought.

This fossil is more than 541 million years old. Some scientists now believe this ancient organism may have lived on land and not in the sea as they first thought.

DESERT SURPRISES

The desert may seem like the last place you'd find the fossil of a marine creature. However, many marine fossils have, in fact, been found in the Sahara Desert in Africa. Ancient marine fossils known as nummulites can be found in the stone blocks that were used to build the Egyptian **pyramids**. These round, single-celled organisms get their name from the word *nummulus*, which means "little coin."

Part of the Sahara Desert is called Wadi al-Hitan, which means "Whale Valley." This name comes from the prehistoric whale fossils that have been found here. Rocks found at Wadi al-Hitan are around 55.8 million to 33.9 million years old. This is about the same age as the stone used to build the pyramids. Many of the fossils here belong to ancient marine creatures.

Dig It!

The Atacama Desert in Chile also has a "whale graveyard" that is full of marine fossils.

Basilosaurus isis

Basilosaurus isis, a type of early whale, lived between 40 million and 34 million years ago. Their fossils have been found at Wadi al-Hitan.

MARINE FOSSILS IN KANSAS?

Today we know Kansas as a mostly dry, flat state in the middle of the United States. So you might be surprised to learn there were once marine animals swimming there. As recently as 80 million years ago, Kansas was covered by a warm, shallow body of water. Fish, turtles, swimming birds, and reptiles called plesiosaurs and mosasaurs lived there. Rocks in Kansas contain fossils of some of these animals, including sharks.

One of the earliest fossil finds in Kansas was made by nine-year-old George F. Sternberg. George visited his father at a dig site in 1892 and found a nearly complete plesiosaur skeleton. Plesiosaurs lived between 228 million and 65 million years ago. George grew up and became a paleontologist, just like his father.

Plesiosaurs lived in both salt water and freshwater. Some types had long necks and short tails, while others had shorter necks and longer tails.

fossil of a *Pteranodon* beak

Dig It!

Kansas has two official types of state fossils. One is *Tylosaurus*, a giant marine lizard. The other is *Pteranodon*, a large flying reptile.

A FISH WITHIN A FISH

Xiphactinus audax was one of the largest and meanest prehistoric fish in the sea. This ancient beast could grow up to 17 feet (5.2 m) long. It was big enough to swallow seabirds and other fish whole. In 1952, paleontologist Walter Sorensen discovered a *Xiphactinus audax* fossil that proved this.

George Sternberg helped to **excavate** this now-famous "fish within a fish" in Gove County, Kansas. This *Xiphactinus audax* likely died soon after swallowing a 6-foot-long (1.8 m) *Gillicus arcuatus* fish whole. It was preserved with its last meal still in its belly. It's the most complete fossil of its kind. Some of *Xiphactinus audax's* teeth were more than 2 inches (5.1 cm) long. Its jaws were similar to those of modern-day piranhas.

Dig It!

In 1982, Dana Bonner found a similar fish-within-a-fish fossil in Kansas. Her fossil also had a *Gillicus arcuatus* within it, but this one was upside down.

24

This *Xiphactinus audax* died shortly after swallowing its meal whole. The fish it ate may have struggled and caused a deadly **internal** injury.

25

SHELL-CRUSHING SHARK

In the early 2000s, paleontologists found a large piece of fossilized jawbone, complete with hundreds of teeth, in Kansas. It took them a full day to remove the fossil from the side of the rocky cliff where it was located. It's believed that the jaw and teeth belong to *Ptychodus mortoni*, an ancient shark that lived about 88.7 million years ago. Paleontologists think there may be more bones and teeth buried in the cliff, but they can't be reached.

Scientists think *Ptychodus mortoni* could grow up to 33 feet (10.1 m) long. It likely had a 3-foot (.9 m) jaw that could crush shelled sea creatures such as giant clams. *Ptychodus mortoni* was big, but it definitely wasn't the biggest ancient shark.

Scientists think that *Ptychodus mortoni* may have looked like a modern-day nurse shark.

rendering of a *Ptychodus mortoni*

modern-day nurse shark

THE FIRST MARINE HERBIVORE

Atopodentatus unicus was a marine reptile that lived about 242 million years ago. Fossils found in southern China's Yunnan Province show that this creature had a strange, T-shaped head with a mouth full of peg-like teeth. Deeper inside its mouth were sharp, needlelike teeth. Despite all these teeth, Atopodentatus unicus may have been the first plant-eating marine reptile. Its front teeth scraped plants off the ocean floor, and its back teeth acted as a filter. Eating plants was very rare for prehistoric marine reptiles.

Paleontologists had a hard time learning about Atopodentatus unicus at first. The fossil they found had been crushed, and it was hard to sort out how the skeleton should have looked. Luckily, more fossils were found, and scientists were able to solve the mystery.

Unlike *Atopodentatus unicus*, mosasaurs were carnivores. This means they ate meat. Mosasaurs had jaws that could open wide. They also had extra teeth to help them swallow prey whole.

rendering of a mosasaur

Dig It!

In the 1800s, American geologist Benjamin Franklin Mudge discovered mosasaurs, plesiosaurs, ancient mollusks, and several types of prehistoric fish.

STUDYING MARINE FOSSILS

Marine fossils offer an important and interesting peek into the past. They give us information about a world that existed many years ago. By studying marine fossils, paleontologists have learned a lot about how organisms that once swam in Earth's ancient seas lived, **evolved**, and went extinct. Scientists have also learned that water once covered many parts of the world—even where tall mountains now stand.

If you're interested in becoming a paleontologist someday, make sure you study science and history in school. You'll likely need a college degree in biology, which is the science of life. It's also helpful to study geology, which is the science of the earth. Keep an eye out for fossils the next time you're playing outside. You might make a great discovery.

GLOSSARY

algae: Plantlike living things without roots or stems that mostly live in water.

ancestor: One of the organisms from which another organism is descended.

decompose: To rot away or break down naturally.

evolve: To grow and change over time.

excavate: To uncover something by digging away and removing the earth that covers it.

frond: A leaf, such as one from a palm tree.

internal: Existing or occurring inside the body.

marine: Having to do with the sea.

organism: An individual living thing.

pyramid: A large, stone structure with a square bottom and triangular sides that meet at a point on top.

INDEX

A
Africa, 20
ammonites, 7
Archaean eon, 9
Atopodentatus unicus,
    28, 29
Australia, 7, 17

B
bacteria, 4, 5, 6
Basilosaurus isis, 21
Bonner, Dana, 24

C
Cambrian period, 14
Chile, 20
China, 28
cephalopods, 15
coral, 16, 17
cyanobacteria, 5

G
Gillicus arcuatus, 24

H
Holocene epoch, 9

I
Indiana, 16

J
Jurassic period, 15

K
Kansas, 4, 22, 23,
    24, 26
Kentucky, 16

M
megalodon, 12, 13
mollusk, 14, 15, 29
Morocco, 14
mosasaur, 22, 29
Mudge, Benjamin
    Franklin, 29

N
Nepal, 7
nummulites, 20

P
Permian period, 17
plesiosaur, 22, 23, 29
Ptychodus mortoni,
    26, 27

S
shark, 12, 13, 22,
    26, 27
Sorensen, Walter, 24
Sternberg, George F.,
    22, 24

T
trilobite, 10, 11
Tylosaurus, 23

U
United States, 22

W
Wadi al-Hitan, 20, 21

X
Xiphactinus audax,
    24, 25

WEBSITES

Due to the changing nature of Internet links, PowerKids
Press has developed an online list of websites related to the
subject of this book. This site is updated regularly. Please use this
link to access the list: www.powerkidslinks.com/ff/marine